WALTER THE EDUCATOR'S LITTLE CHILI RECIPES COOKBOOK

Walter the Educator's Little Chili Recipes Cookbook

Walter the Educator

Silent King Books a WhichHead Imprint

Copyright © 2024 by Walter the Educator

All rights reserved. No part of this book may be reproduced in any manner whatsoever without written permission except in the case of brief quotations embodied in critical articles and reviews.

First Printing, 2024

Disclaimer
This book is for entertainment and informational purposes only. The author and publisher offer this information without warranties expressed or implied. No matter the grounds, neither the author nor the publisher will be accountable for any losses, injuries, or other damages caused by the reader's use of this book. The use of this book acknowledges an understanding and acceptance of this disclaimer.

dedicated to all those that enjoy great food

CONTENTS

Dedication v

One - Walter's Hearty Three-bean Chili 1

Two - Walter's Turkey And Bean Chili 4

Three - Walter's Lemon-garlic Roasted Chicken 7

Four - Walter's Vegan Chili 10

Five - Walter's Cilantro Chili 13

Six - Walter's Queso-infused Chili 15

Seven - Walter's Tomato Chili 18

Eight - Walter's Spicy Chili 20

Nine - Walter's Green Chili 22

Ten - Walter's Black Bean Chili 24

Eleven - Walter's Hawaiian Chili 26

Twelve - Walter's Chili French Fries 28

Thirteen - Walter's Chipotle Chili 30

Fourteen - Walter's Meaty Chili 33

Fifteen - Walter's Taco Chili 36

Sixteen - Walter's Pork Chili 38

Seventeen - Walter's Chili Biscuits 41

Eighteen - Walter's Vegetarian 44

Nineteen - Walter's Red Chili 47

Twenty - Walter's Steak And Chili 50

Twenty-One - Walter's Chili Dogs 52

Twenty-Two - Walter's Italian Sausage Chili 54

Twenty-Three - Walter's Tangy Chili 57

Twenty-Four - Walter's Chili Casserole 60

About The Author 63

ONE

WALTER'S HEARTY THREE-BEAN CHILI

Ingredients:
1 tablespoon olive oil
1 large onion, diced
3 cloves garlic, minced
1 red bell pepper, diced
1 yellow bell pepper, diced
1 jalapeño pepper, finely chopped
1 pound ground beef
1 can (14 oz) diced tomatoes
1 can (14 oz) tomato sauce
1 can (14 oz) black beans, drained and rinsed
1 can (14 oz) kidney beans, drained and rinsed
1 can (14 oz) pinto beans, drained and rinsed
2 cups beef broth
2 tablespoons chili powder

1 tablespoon cumin

1 teaspoon paprika

1 teaspoon oregano

Salt and pepper to taste

Optional toppings: shredded cheddar cheese, sour cream, chopped green onions, cilantro

Instructions:

Heat the olive oil in a large pot over medium heat. Add the diced onion, garlic, and peppers. Sauté for 5-7 minutes until the vegetables are softened.

Add the ground beef to the pot and cook until browned, breaking it up with a spoon as it cooks.

Stir in the diced tomatoes, tomato sauce, black beans, kidney beans, pinto beans, and beef broth.

Add the chili powder, cumin, paprika, oregano, salt, and pepper. Stir to combine all the ingredients.

Bring the chili to a simmer, then reduce the heat and let it simmer for 30-40 minutes, stirring occasionally.

Taste and adjust the seasoning if necessary.

Serve the chili hot, topped with shredded cheddar cheese, a dollop of sour cream, chopped green onions, and fresh cilantro. Enjoy with crusty bread or cornbread.

This hearty three-bean chili is a flavorful and comforting dish that will warm you up on a cold day. The combination of spices, tender beef, and a variety of beans creates a rich and satisfying meal. Whether you're hosting a gathering or simply craving a bowl of delicious chili, this recipe is sure to impress your taste buds and leave you wanting more.

TWO

WALTER'S TURKEY AND BEAN CHILI

Ingredients:
1 tablespoon olive oil
1 large yellow onion, finely chopped
3 cloves garlic, minced
1 red bell pepper, diced
1 yellow bell pepper, diced
1 jalapeño pepper, seeded and minced
1 pound ground turkey
1 can (14 oz) diced tomatoes
1 can (14 oz) tomato sauce
1 can (14 oz) black beans, drained and rinsed
1 can (14 oz) kidney beans, drained and rinsed
2 cups chicken broth
2 tablespoons chili powder
1 tablespoon cumin

1 teaspoon paprika

1 teaspoon dried oregano

Salt and pepper to taste

Optional toppings: shredded cheddar cheese, sour cream, sliced avocado, chopped fresh cilantro

Instructions:

In a large pot, heat the olive oil over medium heat. Add the chopped onion, garlic, and peppers. Cook for 5-7 minutes until the vegetables are softened.

Add the ground turkey to the pot and cook until browned, breaking it up with a spoon as it cooks.

Stir in the diced tomatoes, tomato sauce, black beans, kidney beans, and chicken broth.

Add the chili powder, cumin, paprika, oregano, salt, and pepper. Stir to combine all the ingredients.

Bring the chili to a simmer, then reduce the heat and let it simmer for 25-30 minutes, stirring occasionally.

Taste and adjust the seasoning if necessary.

Serve the turkey chili hot, topped with shredded cheddar cheese, a dollop of sour cream, sliced avocado, and a sprinkle of fresh cilantro. Enjoy with warm cornbread or crusty bread.

This savory turkey and bean chili is a delightful twist on a classic dish, boasting a medley of spices and tender ground turkey. The hearty combination of beans and vegetables creates a satisfying and nourishing meal that's perfect for gatherings or a cozy night in. With its rich flavors and comforting aroma, this chili is sure to be a hit with anyone craving a bowl of heartwarming goodness.

THREE

WALTER'S LEMON-GARLIC ROASTED CHICKEN

Ingredients:
1 whole chicken (about 4-5 pounds)
4 cloves garlic, minced
Zest of 1 lemon
Juice of 1 lemon
3 tablespoons olive oil
1 tablespoon fresh rosemary, chopped
1 tablespoon fresh thyme leaves
1 teaspoon dried oregano
Salt and black pepper to taste
1 lemon, halved
Fresh herbs for garnish (rosemary, thyme, parsley)
Instructions:

Preheat the oven to 425°F (220°C).

In a small bowl, mix the minced garlic, lemon zest, lemon juice, olive oil, chopped rosemary, thyme, and oregano to create a marinade.

Pat the chicken dry with paper towels and season the cavity with salt and pepper.

Carefully loosen the skin of the chicken from the meat. Spoon half of the marinade mixture under the skin, spreading it evenly over the breast and thigh meat.

Rub the remaining marinade all over the outside of the chicken. Season the entire chicken generously with salt and pepper.

Place the halved lemon and a few sprigs of fresh herbs inside the cavity of the chicken.

Truss the chicken with kitchen twine and tuck the wings underneath the body.

Place the chicken on a roasting pan or oven-safe skillet and roast in the preheated oven for 1 hour to 1 hour and 15 minutes, or until the internal temperature reaches 165°F (74°C) in the thickest part of the thigh.

Once cooked, remove the chicken from the oven and let it rest for 10-15 minutes before carving.

Garnish with fresh herbs and serve the succulent lemon-garlic roasted chicken with your favorite sides.

This succulent lemon-garlic roasted chicken is a showstopper, bursting with vibrant flavors and juicy tenderness. The zesty marinade infuses the meat with a delightful aroma, complemented by the earthy notes of fresh herbs. Whether it's a special occasion or a comforting family dinner, this recipe is sure to impress with its savory appeal and mouthwatering appeal.

FOUR

WALTER'S VEGAN CHILI

Ingredients:
2 tablespoons olive oil
1 large onion, diced
3 cloves garlic, minced
1 red bell pepper, diced
1 green bell pepper, diced
2 carrots, diced
1 zucchini, diced
1 cup corn kernels
1 can (15 oz) black beans, drained and rinsed
1 can (15 oz) kidney beans, drained and rinsed
1 can (15 oz) chickpeas, drained and rinsed
1 can (28 oz) diced tomatoes
1 cup vegetable broth
2 tablespoons chili powder

1 tablespoon cumin

1 teaspoon paprika

1 teaspoon oregano

Salt and pepper to taste

Optional toppings: sliced avocado, chopped fresh cilantro, lime wedges

Instructions:

In a large pot, heat the olive oil over medium heat. Add the diced onion, garlic, bell peppers, carrots, and zucchini. Sauté for 5-7 minutes until the vegetables are softened.

Add the corn, black beans, kidney beans, chickpeas, diced tomatoes, and vegetable broth to the pot.

Stir in the chili powder, cumin, paprika, oregano, salt, and pepper. Mix well to combine all the ingredients.

Bring the vegan chili to a simmer, then reduce the heat and let it simmer for 25-30 minutes, stirring occasionally.

Taste and adjust the seasoning if necessary.

Serve the vegan chili hot, topped with sliced avocado, chopped fresh cilantro, and a squeeze of lime juice. Enjoy with crusty bread or rice.

This vibrant vegan chili is a delightful medley of colorful vegetables and hearty beans, bursting with robust flavors and wholesome goodness. The combination of aromatic spices and nourishing ingredients creates a satisfying and nutritious meal that's perfect for any occasion. Whether you follow a vegan lifestyle or simply enjoy plant-based cuisine, this recipe is a tantalizing option that promises to tantalize your taste buds and leave you craving more.

FIVE

WALTER'S CILANTRO CHILI

Ingredients for Cilantro Chili:
1 pound ground beef
1 onion, diced
3 cloves garlic, minced
1 red bell pepper, diced
1 can (14 oz) diced tomatoes
1 can (14 oz) tomato sauce
1 can (14 oz) black beans, drained and rinsed
1 can (14 oz) kidney beans, drained and rinsed
2 cups beef broth
2 tablespoons chili powder
1 tablespoon ground cumin
1 teaspoon paprika
Salt and pepper to taste

1/2 cup chopped fresh cilantro

Steps to Prepare Cilantro Chili:

In a large pot or Dutch oven, brown the ground beef over medium heat, breaking it up with a spoon as it cooks.

Add the diced onion, minced garlic, and diced red bell pepper to the pot. Sauté for 5-7 minutes until the vegetables are softened.

Stir in the diced tomatoes, tomato sauce, black beans, kidney beans, and beef broth.

Add the chili powder, cumin, paprika, salt, and pepper. Mix well to combine all the ingredients.

Bring the cilantro chili to a simmer, then reduce the heat and let it simmer for 25-30 minutes, stirring occasionally.

Taste and adjust the seasoning if necessary.

Just before serving, stir in the chopped fresh cilantro to infuse the chili with its vibrant flavor.

Serve the cilantro chili hot, topped with a dollop of sour cream, shredded cheese, and additional fresh cilantro for garnish. Enjoy with cornbread or crusty bread.

This cilantro-infused chili is a tantalizing blend of savory beef, aromatic spices, and the fresh, citrusy essence of cilantro. It's a delightful twist on a classic chili recipe, promising to elevate your taste buds to new heights of satisfaction and enjoyment.

SIX

WALTER'S QUESO-INFUSED CHILI

Ingredients:
1 pound ground beef
1 onion, diced
3 cloves garlic, minced
1 can (14 ounces) diced tomatoes
1 can (14 ounces) black beans, drained and rinsed
1 can (14 ounces) kidney beans, drained and rinsed
1 can (14 ounces) corn kernels, drained
1 cup beef broth
1 tablespoon chili powder
1 teaspoon cumin
1 teaspoon paprika
Salt and pepper to taste

1 cup queso cheese dip

Optional toppings: chopped cilantro, sliced jalapeños, sour cream, tortilla chips

Steps:

In a large pot or Dutch oven, brown the ground beef over medium heat. Add the diced onion and minced garlic, and cook until the onion is soft and translucent.

Stir in the diced tomatoes, black beans, kidney beans, and corn kernels. Pour in the beef broth and stir to combine.

Add the chili powder, cumin, paprika, salt, and pepper. Mix well and bring the chili to a simmer.

Let the chili simmer for 20-25 minutes, stirring occasionally.

Once the chili is cooked and the flavors have melded, stir in the queso cheese dip until it's fully incorporated and melted into the chili.

Serve the queso chili hot, topped with optional toppings such as chopped cilantro, sliced jalapeños, a dollop of sour cream, and a side of tortilla chips for dipping.

This queso-infused chili is a delightful fusion of hearty beef, beans, and vibrant spices, all brought together with the creamy richness of queso cheese. It's a mouthwatering twist on traditional chili, guaranteed to impress with its bold flavors and indulgent appeal. Whether it's a game day gathering or a cozy night in, this recipe promises to elevate your chili experience to a whole new level of deliciousness.

SEVEN

WALTER'S TOMATO CHILI

Ingredients:
1 pound ground beef
1 onion, diced
3 cloves garlic, minced
1 can (28 ounces) crushed tomatoes
1 can (15 ounces) kidney beans, drained and rinsed
1 can (15 ounces) black beans, drained and rinsed
1 can (15 ounces) diced tomatoes
2 tablespoons tomato paste
2 teaspoons chili powder
1 teaspoon cumin
1 teaspoon paprika
1/2 teaspoon oregano
Salt and pepper, to taste
Optional toppings: shredded cheddar cheese, sour

cream, sliced green onions, diced avocado, fresh cilantro

Steps:

In a large pot or Dutch oven, brown the ground beef over medium heat until fully cooked. Drain any excess fat.

Add the diced onion and minced garlic to the pot and sauté until the onion is translucent and fragrant.

Stir in the crushed tomatoes, diced tomatoes, tomato paste, kidney beans, black beans, chili powder, cumin, paprika, oregano, salt, and pepper. Mix well to combine all the ingredients.

Bring the tomato chili to a simmer, then reduce the heat and let it simmer for 25-30 minutes, stirring occasionally.

Taste and adjust the seasoning if necessary.

Serve the tomato chili hot, topped with shredded cheddar cheese, a dollop of sour cream, sliced green onions, diced avocado, and a sprinkle of fresh cilantro. Enjoy with warm cornbread or crusty bread.

This robust tomato chili is a tantalizing blend of savory beef, aromatic spices, and the rich, tangy essence of tomatoes. It's a comforting and satisfying dish that promises to warm you up from the inside out, with each spoonful bursting with flavor. Whether it's a casual weeknight dinner or a gathering with friends, this recipe is sure to delight your taste buds and leave you craving more of its mouthwatering goodness.

EIGHT

WALTER'S SPICY CHILI

Ingredients:
1 lb ground beef
1 onion, diced
3 cloves garlic, minced
1 bell pepper, diced
1 can (14 oz) diced tomatoes
1 can (14 oz) tomato sauce
1 can (14 oz) kidney beans, drained and rinsed
1 can (14 oz) black beans, drained and rinsed
1 cup beef broth
2 tablespoons chili powder
1 teaspoon cumin
1 teaspoon paprika
1/2 teaspoon cayenne pepper (adjust to taste for more or less heat)

Salt and pepper to taste

Chopped fresh cilantro and sliced jalapeños for garnish

Instructions:

In a large pot or Dutch oven, brown the ground beef over medium-high heat. Add the diced onion, minced garlic, and diced bell pepper, and cook until the vegetables are tender and the beef is browned.

Stir in the diced tomatoes, tomato sauce, drained and rinsed kidney beans, drained and rinsed black beans, and beef broth.

Add the chili powder, cumin, paprika, cayenne pepper, salt, and pepper. Stir well to combine all the ingredients.

Bring the chili to a simmer, then reduce the heat to low. Let the chili simmer for 30-40 minutes, stirring occasionally.

Taste and adjust the seasoning if necessary, adding more cayenne pepper for extra heat if desired.

Serve the spicy chili hot, garnished with chopped fresh cilantro, and sliced jalapeños for an extra kick. Enjoy with your favorite toppings and sides, such as shredded cheese, sour cream, and cornbread.

This spicy chili is a flavor-packed delight, perfect for warming up on a cold day or for adding a fiery kick to your meal. The blend of aromatic spices and hearty ingredients creates a satisfying dish that's sure to tantalize your taste buds and leave you reaching for seconds.

NINE

WALTER'S GREEN CHILI

Ingredients:
2 lbs boneless, skinless chicken thighs
1 tablespoon olive oil
1 onion, diced
4 cloves garlic, minced
2 cans (4 oz each) diced green chilies
1 lb fresh tomatillos, husks removed and diced
1 jalapeño, seeded and diced
1 teaspoon ground cumin
1 teaspoon dried oregano
4 cups chicken broth
Salt and pepper to taste
Fresh cilantro, for garnish
Steps:
In a large pot, heat the olive oil over medium

heat. Add the diced onion and garlic, and sauté until softened.

Add the chicken thighs to the pot and cook until browned on all sides.

Stir in the diced green chilies, tomatillos, jalapeño, ground cumin, and dried oregano. Cook for a few minutes to allow the flavors to meld.

Pour in the chicken broth and bring the mixture to a simmer. Cover the pot and let it cook for about 30-40 minutes, or until the chicken is cooked through and tender.

Once the chicken is cooked, remove it from the pot and shred it using two forks. Return the shredded chicken to the pot and stir to combine.

Season the green chili with salt and pepper to taste.

Serve the green chili hot, garnished with chopped fresh cilantro. Enjoy with warm tortillas or rice.

This green chili is a delightful and unique addition to your recipe collection, offering a burst of fresh flavors and a satisfying warmth that's perfect for any occasion.

TEN

WALTER'S BLACK BEAN CHILI

Ingredients:
1 lb ground beef
1 onion, diced
3 cloves garlic, minced
2 (15 oz) cans black beans, drained and rinsed
1 (15 oz) can diced tomatoes
1 cup beef broth
1 tablespoon chili powder
1 teaspoon cumin
1 teaspoon smoked paprika
1/2 teaspoon oregano
Salt and pepper to taste
Optional toppings: shredded cheddar cheese, sour cream, chopped green onions, fresh cilantro
Instructions:

In a large pot or Dutch oven, brown the ground beef over medium heat until fully cooked. Drain any excess fat.

Add the diced onion and minced garlic to the pot, and cook until the onion is translucent.

Stir in the black beans, diced tomatoes, and beef broth.

Add the chili powder, cumin, smoked paprika, oregano, salt, and pepper. Stir to combine.

Bring the chili to a simmer, then reduce the heat to low and let it simmer for about 20-30 minutes, stirring occasionally.

Taste and adjust the seasoning if needed.

Serve the chili hot, topped with shredded cheddar cheese, a dollop of sour cream, chopped green onions, and fresh cilantro. Enjoy with crusty bread or cornbread.

This black bean chili is a perfect balance of rich flavors and hearty ingredients, making it a crowd-pleasing favorite for any gathering or a cozy night in.

ELEVEN

WALTER'S HAWAIIAN CHILI

Ingredients:
1 pound ground beef
1 onion, diced
1 red bell pepper, diced
1 can (14 ounces) crushed pineapple
1 can (15 ounces) kidney beans, drained and rinsed
1 can (15 ounces) black beans, drained and rinsed
1 can (28 ounces) diced tomatoes
1 cup pineapple juice
2 tablespoons soy sauce
3 cloves garlic, minced
2 teaspoons chili powder
1 teaspoon ground ginger
1 teaspoon paprika
Salt and pepper to taste

Sliced green onions and chopped cilantro for garnish
Steps:

In a large pot or Dutch oven, brown the ground beef over medium heat until fully cooked. Drain any excess fat.

Add the diced onion and red bell pepper to the pot and cook until they begin to soften.

Stir in the crushed pineapple (including the juice), kidney beans, black beans, diced tomatoes, and pineapple juice.

Add the soy sauce, minced garlic, chili powder, ground ginger, and paprika to the pot. Stir to combine all the ingredients.

Season the chili with salt and pepper to taste.

Bring the chili to a simmer and let it cook for 20-30 minutes, allowing the flavors to meld together.

Once the chili is ready, ladle it into bowls and garnish with sliced green onions and chopped cilantro.

Serve the Hawaiian chili hot and enjoy with a side of rice or your favorite Hawaiian bread.

This Hawaiian chili is a delightful fusion of sweet and savory flavors, offering a taste of the islands in every spoonful. It's a perfect dish for bringing a touch of tropical flair to your table and is sure to be a hit with family and friends.

TWELVE

WALTER'S CHILI FRENCH FRIES

Ingredients:

- 1 pound of frozen French fries
- 1 can of chili (homemade or store-bought)
- Shredded cheddar cheese
- Sliced jalapeños
- Chopped green onions
- Sour cream

Steps:

1. Preheat your oven and bake the French fries according to the package instructions until they are golden and crispy.
2. While the fries are baking, heat the chili in a

saucepan over medium heat until it's hot and bubbly.
3. Once the fries are done, transfer them to a serving platter or individual plates.
4. Spoon the hot chili over the crispy fries, ensuring that each fry is generously coated.
5. Sprinkle shredded cheddar cheese over the chili-covered fries, allowing it to melt and create a gooey, delicious topping.
6. Garnish the chili fries with sliced jalapeños, chopped green onions, and a dollop of sour cream for an extra kick and creamy finish.
7. Serve the mouthwatering chili French fries hot and enjoy the delightful combination of crispy, savory, and cheesy flavors.

These chili French fries are a crowd-pleasing indulgence, perfect for game day gatherings, casual get-togethers, or simply when you're craving a delicious and satisfying treat.

THIRTEEN

WALTER'S CHIPOTLE CHILI

Ingredients:

- 2 pounds ground beef
- 1 onion, diced
- 4 cloves garlic, minced
- 2 cans (14 oz) diced tomatoes
- 1 can (14 oz) tomato sauce
- 2 cans (14 oz) kidney beans, drained and rinsed
- 2 chipotle peppers in adobo sauce, minced
- 2 tablespoons adobo sauce
- 2 tablespoons chili powder
- 1 teaspoon cumin
- 1 teaspoon paprika
- Salt and pepper to taste
- 2 cups beef broth

- Olive oil

Steps:

1. In a large pot or Dutch oven, heat a drizzle of olive oil over medium heat. Add the diced onion and minced garlic, and sauté until softened and fragrant.
2. Add the ground beef to the pot, breaking it up with a spoon, and cook until browned and cooked through.
3. Stir in the diced tomatoes, tomato sauce, kidney beans, minced chipotle peppers, adobo sauce, chili powder, cumin, paprika, salt, and pepper. Mix well to combine.
4. Pour in the beef broth and bring the chili to a simmer. Let it cook for about 30-40 minutes, stirring occasionally, until the flavors have melded together and the chili has thickened to your desired consistency.
5. Taste and adjust the seasoning if needed.
6. Serve the chipotle chili hot, garnished with chopped fresh cilantro and a dollop of sour cream. Enjoy with your favorite sides, such as rice, cornbread, or tortilla chips.

This chipotle chili is a smoky, spicy, and savory delight, perfect for adding a kick of flavor to your meal. It's a hearty and satisfying dish that promises to tantalize your taste buds and leave you craving more of its mouthwatering goodness.

FOURTEEN

WALTER'S MEATY CHILI

Ingredients:

- 1 pound ground beef
- 1 pound ground pork
- 1 onion, diced
- 3 cloves garlic, minced
- 1 bell pepper, diced
- 1 can (14 oz) diced tomatoes
- 1 can (14 oz) tomato sauce
- 1 can (14 oz) kidney beans, drained and rinsed
- 1 can (14 oz) black beans, drained and rinsed
- 2 tablespoons chili powder
- 1 teaspoon cumin
- 1 teaspoon smoked paprika
- Salt and pepper to taste

- Optional toppings: shredded cheddar cheese, sour cream, chopped green onions

Steps:

1. In a large pot or Dutch oven, brown the ground beef and ground pork over medium-high heat until fully cooked. Drain any excess fat.
2. Add the diced onion, minced garlic, and diced bell pepper to the pot. Cook for a few minutes until the vegetables have softened.
3. Stir in the diced tomatoes, tomato sauce, kidney beans, black beans, chili powder, cumin, and smoked paprika.
4. Bring the chili to a simmer, then reduce the heat to low. Cover and let it simmer for about 30-40 minutes, stirring occasionally.
5. Taste and adjust the seasoning with salt and pepper if needed.
6. Serve the meaty chili hot, topped with shredded cheddar cheese, a dollop of sour cream, and chopped green onions. Enjoy with a side of cornbread or crusty bread.

This meaty chili is a hearty and satisfying dish, perfect for warming up on a cold day or for serving to a hungry crowd. The combination of savory meats, aromatic spices, and beans creates a flavorful and mouthwatering chili that's sure to be a hit at any gathering.

FIFTEEN

WALTER'S TACO CHILI

Ingredients:

- 1 pound ground beef
- 1 onion, diced
- 1 bell pepper, diced
- 3 cloves garlic, minced
- 1 can (15 oz) black beans, drained and rinsed
- 1 can (15 oz) kidney beans, drained and rinsed
- 1 can (15 oz) corn, drained
- 1 can (15 oz) diced tomatoes
- 1 can (8 oz) tomato sauce
- 1 packet taco seasoning
- 2 cups beef broth
- Salt and pepper to taste
- Toppings: shredded cheese, sour cream, sliced jalapeños, chopped cilantro, tortilla chips

Steps:

1. In a large pot or Dutch oven, brown the ground beef over medium heat. Drain any excess fat.
2. Add the diced onion, bell pepper, and garlic to the pot. Cook until the vegetables are softened.
3. Stir in the black beans, kidney beans, corn, diced tomatoes, tomato sauce, and taco seasoning.
4. Pour in the beef broth and stir to combine all the ingredients.
5. Bring the chili to a simmer and let it cook for about 20-30 minutes, stirring occasionally.
6. Taste and adjust the seasoning with salt and pepper, if needed.
7. Serve the taco chili hot, topped with shredded cheese, a dollop of sour cream, sliced jalapeños, and chopped cilantro. Enjoy with a side of tortilla chips for dipping.

This taco chili is a mouthwatering fusion of classic chili flavors and vibrant taco spices, offering a delightful twist on traditional chili. It's a satisfying and flavorful dish that's perfect for gatherings or cozy nights in, promising to impress with its bold and delicious appeal.

SIXTEEN

WALTER'S PORK CHILI

Ingredients:

- 2 pounds pork shoulder, trimmed and cut into cubes
- 1 onion, diced
- 4 cloves garlic, minced
- 2 cans (14 oz) diced tomatoes
- 1 can (14 oz) black beans, drained and rinsed
- 1 can (14 oz) kidney beans, drained and rinsed
- 1 cup chicken broth
- 2 tablespoons chili powder
- 1 tablespoon cumin
- 1 teaspoon paprika
- Salt and pepper to taste
- Chopped fresh cilantro for garnish

Steps:

1. In a large pot or Dutch oven, brown the pork cubes over medium-high heat until they are golden and crispy. Remove the pork from the pot and set aside.
2. In the same pot, add the diced onion and cook until it becomes translucent. Add the minced garlic and cook for another minute.
3. Return the browned pork to the pot, and add the diced tomatoes, black beans, kidney beans, chicken broth, chili powder, cumin, paprika, salt, and pepper. Stir to combine all the ingredients.
4. Bring the chili to a boil, then reduce the heat to a simmer. Cover the pot and let the chili cook for about 1.5 to 2 hours, stirring occasionally, until the pork is tender and the flavors have melded together.
5. Once the pork chili is ready, taste and adjust the seasoning if needed.
6. Serve the mouthwatering pork chili hot, garnished with chopped fresh cilantro. Enjoy with a side of warm tortillas or rice.

This mouthwatering pork chili is a hearty and flavorful dish, perfect for warming up on a cold day or for serving to a hungry crowd. The combination of succulent pork, aromatic spices, and beans creates a satisfying and delicious chili that's sure to be a hit at any gathering.

SEVENTEEN

WALTER'S CHILI BISCUITS

Ingredients: For the chili:

- 1 pound ground beef
- 1 onion, diced
- 2 cloves garlic, minced
- 1 can (14 oz) diced tomatoes
- 1 can (14 oz) kidney beans, drained and rinsed
- 1 can (6 oz) tomato paste
- 1 cup beef broth
- 1 tablespoon chili powder
- 1 teaspoon cumin
- Salt and pepper to taste

For the biscuits:

- 2 cups all-purpose flour
- 1 tablespoon baking powder
- 1/2 teaspoon salt
- 1/2 cup unsalted butter, cold and cubed
- 3/4 cup buttermilk
- 1/2 cup shredded cheddar cheese
- 2 tablespoons chopped fresh parsley

Steps:

1. In a large pot, brown the ground beef over medium heat. Add the diced onion and garlic, and cook until the onion is softened and the beef is browned.
2. Stir in the diced tomatoes, kidney beans, tomato paste, beef broth, chili powder, cumin, salt, and pepper. Bring the mixture to a simmer, then reduce the heat and let it simmer for about 20-30 minutes, stirring occasionally.
3. Preheat the oven to 400°F (200°C).
4. In a large bowl, whisk together the flour, baking powder, and salt. Cut in the cold, cubed butter using a pastry cutter or fork until the mixture resembles coarse crumbs.
5. Stir in the buttermilk, cheddar cheese, and chopped parsley until just combined.
6. Drop spoonfuls of the biscuit dough on top of the simmering chili in the pot.
7. Transfer the pot to the preheated oven and

bake for 20-25 minutes, or until the biscuits are golden brown and the chili is bubbly.
8. Serve the mouthwatering chili biscuits hot and enjoy the delightful combination of savory chili and fluffy, cheesy biscuits.

This mouthwatering chili biscuits recipe is a comforting and satisfying meal that's perfect for cozy nights in or for sharing with friends and family.

EIGHTEEN

WALTER'S VEGETARIAN

Ingredients:

- 2 tablespoons olive oil
- 1 large onion, diced
- 3 garlic cloves, minced
- 1 red bell pepper, diced
- 1 green bell pepper, diced
- 2 carrots, diced
- 1 zucchini, diced
- 1 cup corn kernels
- 1 can (15 oz) black beans, drained and rinsed
- 1 can (15 oz) kidney beans, drained and rinsed
- 1 can (28 oz) diced tomatoes
- 2 cups vegetable broth
- 2 tablespoons chili powder

- 1 tablespoon cumin
- 1 teaspoon paprika
- 1 teaspoon oregano
- Salt and pepper to taste
- Chopped fresh cilantro for garnish

Steps:

1. In a large pot, heat the olive oil over medium heat. Add the diced onion and garlic, and sauté until the onion is translucent.
2. Add the diced bell peppers, carrots, and zucchini to the pot, and cook for 5-7 minutes, or until the vegetables begin to soften.
3. Stir in the corn, black beans, kidney beans, diced tomatoes, vegetable broth, chili powder, cumin, paprika, oregano, salt, and pepper.
4. Bring the chili to a simmer, then reduce the heat to low and let it simmer for 20-25 minutes, stirring occasionally.
5. Taste and adjust the seasoning if needed.
6. Serve the vegetarian chili hot, garnished with chopped fresh cilantro. Enjoy with a side of warm tortillas or rice.

This mouthwatering vegetarian chili is a hearty and flavorful dish, perfect for warming up on a cold day or for serving to a hungry crowd. The combination of vibrant vegetables, aromatic spices, and beans creates a satisfying and delicious chili that's sure to be a hit at any gathering.

NINETEEN

WALTER'S RED CHILI

Ingredients:

- 2 pounds of beef chuck, cut into cubes
- 2 tablespoons of vegetable oil
- 1 large onion, finely chopped
- 4 cloves of garlic, minced
- 2 red bell peppers, diced
- 2 tablespoons of tomato paste
- 1 can (28 ounces) of crushed tomatoes
- 1 can (15 ounces) of kidney beans, drained and rinsed
- 1 can (15 ounces) of black beans, drained and rinsed
- 3 cups of beef broth
- 2 tablespoons of chili powder
- 1 tablespoon of cumin

- 1 teaspoon of paprika
- Salt and pepper to taste
- Chopped fresh cilantro for garnish

Steps:

1. In a large pot, heat the vegetable oil over medium-high heat. Add the beef cubes and brown them on all sides. Remove the beef from the pot and set it aside.
2. In the same pot, add the chopped onion, garlic, and red bell peppers. Sauté until the vegetables are softened.
3. Stir in the tomato paste and cook for a minute to enhance the flavor.
4. Return the browned beef to the pot and add the crushed tomatoes, kidney beans, black beans, beef broth, chili powder, cumin, and paprika. Stir to combine.
5. Bring the chili to a boil, then reduce the heat to low and let it simmer for about 2 hours, stirring occasionally.
6. Taste and adjust the seasoning with salt and pepper if needed.
7. Serve the mouthwatering red chili hot, garnished with chopped fresh cilantro. Enjoy with a side of warm tortillas or rice.

This mouthwatering red chili is a rich and flavorful

dish, perfect for warming up on a cold day or for serving to a hungry crowd. The combination of tender beef, aromatic spices, and hearty beans creates a satisfying and delicious chili that's sure to be a hit at any gathering.

TWENTY

WALTER'S STEAK AND CHILI

Ingredients:

- 1 1/2 pounds of steak, cut into cubes
- 1 onion, diced
- 3 cloves of garlic, minced
- 1 red bell pepper, diced
- 1 can of diced tomatoes
- 1 can of kidney beans, drained and rinsed
- 2 cups of beef broth
- 2 tablespoons of tomato paste
- 2 tablespoons of chili powder
- 1 tablespoon of cumin
- 1 teaspoon of paprika
- Salt and pepper to taste
- Chopped fresh cilantro for garnish

Steps:

1. In a large pot or Dutch oven, heat some oil over medium-high heat. Add the steak cubes and cook until browned on all sides. Remove the steak from the pot and set aside.
2. In the same pot, add the diced onion, garlic, and red bell pepper. Cook until the vegetables are softened.
3. Stir in the tomato paste, chili powder, cumin, and paprika, and cook for another minute to toast the spices.
4. Add the diced tomatoes, kidney beans, and beef broth to the pot. Bring the mixture to a simmer.
5. Return the browned steak to the pot, and let the chili simmer for 1-2 hours, stirring occasionally, until the steak is tender and the flavors have melded together.
6. Season with salt and pepper to taste.
7. Serve the mouthwatering steak and chili hot, garnished with chopped fresh cilantro. Enjoy with a side of warm tortillas or rice.

This mouthwatering steak and chili is a hearty and satisfying dish that combines tender steak with rich and flavorful chili. It's perfect for warming up on a cold day or for sharing with friends and family.

TWENTY-ONE

WALTER'S CHILI DOGS

For the chili:

- 1 pound ground beef
- 1 small onion, diced
- 2 cloves garlic, minced
- 1 can (14 ounces) tomato sauce
- 1 can (14 ounces) diced tomatoes
- 2 tablespoons chili powder
- 1 teaspoon cumin
- 1 teaspoon paprika
- Salt and pepper to taste

For the chili dogs:

- 8 hot dog buns
- 8 hot dogs

- 1 cup shredded cheddar cheese
- Diced onions, for garnish
- Mustard and ketchup, for serving

Steps:

1. In a large skillet, cook the ground beef over medium heat until browned. Add the diced onion and garlic, and cook until the onion is softened.
2. Stir in the tomato sauce, diced tomatoes, chili powder, cumin, paprika, salt, and pepper. Simmer the chili for 15-20 minutes, allowing the flavors to meld together.
3. Meanwhile, grill or heat the hot dogs according to package instructions.
4. To assemble the chili dogs, place a grilled hot dog in each bun. Ladle the chili over the hot dogs and sprinkle with shredded cheddar cheese.
5. Garnish with diced onions and serve with mustard and ketchup on the side.

These mouthwatering chili dogs are a delightful combination of savory chili, juicy hot dogs, and flavorful toppings, perfect for a casual gathering or a fun family meal. Enjoy the satisfying flavors and the hearty comfort of this classic dish.

TWENTY-TWO

WALTER'S ITALIAN SAUSAGE CHILI

Ingredients:

- 1 pound Italian sausage, casings removed
- 1 onion, diced
- 3 cloves garlic, minced
- 1 red bell pepper, diced
- 1 can (28 ounces) diced tomatoes
- 1 can (15 ounces) tomato sauce
- 1 can (15 ounces) kidney beans, drained and rinsed
- 1 can (15 ounces) cannellini beans, drained and rinsed
- 1 cup beef broth
- 2 teaspoons Italian seasoning
- 1 teaspoon paprika

- 1 teaspoon dried oregano
- 1/2 teaspoon red pepper flakes
- Salt and pepper to taste
- Grated Parmesan cheese, for serving
- Fresh basil, chopped, for garnish

Steps:

1. In a large pot or Dutch oven, cook the Italian sausage over medium heat, breaking it up with a spoon as it cooks, until browned and cooked through.
2. Add the diced onion, garlic, and red bell pepper to the pot, and cook until the vegetables are softened, about 5 minutes.
3. Stir in the diced tomatoes, tomato sauce, kidney beans, cannellini beans, beef broth, Italian seasoning, paprika, dried oregano, and red pepper flakes.
4. Bring the chili to a simmer, then reduce the heat to low and let it simmer for 30-40 minutes, stirring occasionally.
5. Taste and adjust the seasoning with salt and pepper if needed.
6. Serve the mouthwatering Italian sausage chili hot, garnished with grated Parmesan cheese and chopped fresh basil. Enjoy with a side of crusty bread or garlic bread to soak up the delicious flavors.

This Italian sausage chili is a savory and comforting dish that's perfect for a cozy dinner or for sharing with loved ones. The aromatic herbs, tender sausage, and hearty beans come together to create a robust and flavorful chili that will surely become a new favorite in your recipe collection.

TWENTY-THREE

WALTER'S TANGY CHILI

Ingredients:

- 1 pound ground beef
- 1 onion, diced
- 3 cloves garlic, minced
- 1 bell pepper, diced
- 1 can (15 oz) kidney beans, drained and rinsed
- 1 can (15 oz) black beans, drained and rinsed
- 1 can (28 oz) crushed tomatoes
- 2 tablespoons tomato paste
- 2 tablespoons chili powder
- 1 teaspoon cumin
- 1 teaspoon paprika
- 1 tablespoon brown sugar
- 2 tablespoons apple cider vinegar

- Salt and pepper to taste
- Optional toppings: shredded cheddar cheese, sour cream, chopped green onions

Steps:

1. In a large pot or Dutch oven, brown the ground beef over medium heat until fully cooked. Drain any excess fat.
2. Add the diced onion, minced garlic, and bell pepper to the pot. Cook for 5-7 minutes, or until the vegetables are softened.
3. Stir in the drained and rinsed kidney beans, black beans, crushed tomatoes, and tomato paste.
4. Add the chili powder, cumin, paprika, brown sugar, and apple cider vinegar to the pot. Stir to combine all the ingredients.
5. Season the chili with salt and pepper to taste. Allow the chili to simmer for 20-30 minutes, stirring occasionally.
6. Serve the mouthwatering tangy chili hot, garnished with your choice of toppings such as shredded cheddar cheese, sour cream, and chopped green onions.

This tangy chili is a flavorful and satisfying dish, perfect for warming up on a chilly evening or for sharing with friends and family. The combination of savory beef, zesty tomatoes, and tangy vinegar creates a delightful twist on classic chili that's sure to become a favorite in your recipe repertoire.

TWENTY-FOUR

WALTER'S CHILI CASSEROLE

Ingredients:

- 1 pound ground beef
- 1 onion, diced
- 2 cloves garlic, minced
- 1 can (15 ounces) kidney beans, drained and rinsed
- 1 can (15 ounces) black beans, drained and rinsed
- 1 can (15 ounces) corn kernels, drained
- 1 can (15 ounces) diced tomatoes
- 1 can (8 ounces) tomato sauce
- 2 tablespoons chili powder
- 1 teaspoon cumin
- Salt and pepper to taste
- 2 cups shredded cheddar cheese

- 1 cup crushed tortilla chips
- Chopped fresh cilantro for garnish

Steps:

1. Preheat the oven to 375°F (190°C).
2. In a large skillet, cook the ground beef over medium heat until browned. Add the diced onion and minced garlic, and cook until the onion is translucent.
3. Stir in the kidney beans, black beans, corn, diced tomatoes, and tomato sauce. Add the chili powder, cumin, salt, and pepper. Mix well and let the chili simmer for 10-15 minutes.
4. Transfer the chili mixture to a greased 9x13 inch baking dish. Spread it out evenly.
5. Sprinkle the shredded cheddar cheese over the chili.
6. Top the cheese with the crushed tortilla chips, creating an even layer.
7. Bake the chili casserole in the preheated oven for 25-30 minutes, or until the cheese is melted and bubbly.
8. Garnish with chopped fresh cilantro before serving.

This mouthwatering chili casserole is a delightful and comforting dish that combines the flavors of a classic chili with the satisfying heartiness of a casserole. The layers of savory chili, gooey cheese, and crispy tortilla chips create a delicious and satisfying meal that's perfect for sharing with friends and family.

ABOUT THE AUTHOR

Walter the Educator is one of the pseudonyms for Walter Anderson. Formally educated in Chemistry, Business, and Education, he is an educator, an author, a diverse entrepreneur, and he is the son of a disabled war veteran. "Walter the Educator" shares his time between educating and creating. He holds interests and owns several creative projects that entertain, enlighten, enhance, and educate, hoping to inspire and motivate you.

Follow, find new works, and stay up to date
with Walter the Educator™
at WaltertheEducator.com

www.ingramcontent.com/pod-product-compliance
Lightning Source LLC
LaVergne TN
LVHW052003060526
838201LV00059B/3806